ORIGAMI SAFARI

Ocean Animals

By Ruth Owen

WINDMILL
BOOKS

New York

Published in 2015 by Windmill Books, An Imprint of Rosen Publishing
29 East 21st Street, New York, NY 10010

First Edition

Produced for Rosen by Ruby Tuesday Books Ltd
Editor for Ruby Tuesday Books Ltd: Mark J. Sachner
US Editor: Joshua Shadowens
Designer: Emma Randall

Photo Credits:
Cover, 1, 3, 5, 6–7, 8–9, 10–11, 12–13, 14–15, 16–17, 18–19, 20–21, 22–23, 24–25, 26–27, 28–29, 31 © Ruby Tuesday Books; cover, 4–5, 6, 10, 14, 18, 22, 26 © Shutterstock.

Library of Congress Cataloging-in-Publication Data

Owen, Ruth, 1967– author.
 Ocean animals / By Ruth Owen. — First Edition.
    pages cm. — (Origami safari)
 Includes index.
 ISBN 978-1-4777-9249-0 (library binding) —
ISBN 978-1-4777-9250-6 (pbk.) — ISBN 978-1-4777-9251-3 (6-pack)
1. Origami—Juvenile literature. 2. Marine animals in art—Juvenile
literature. 3. Animals in art—Juvenile literature. I. Title.
 TT872.5.O938 2015
 736.982—dc23

                              2014013966

Manufactured in the United States of America

CPSIA Compliance Information: Batch #WS14WM: For Further Information contact Windmill Books, New York, New York at 1-866-478-0556

Contents

Ocean Origami

About 71 percent of Earth's surface is covered with oceans. Some oceans are warm while others are so cold they have ice floating in them.

Whether warm, cold, deep, or shallow, this watery **habitat** is home to thousands of different types of animals, including **mammals**, fish, and even **reptiles**.

In this book you can read about six animals that live in the ocean. You will also get the chance to make an **origami** model of each animal.

All you need is some colorful, square paper, and you will be ready to follow the step-by-step instructions to make your own collection of origami ocean animals.

A sea turtle swimming with tropical fish

Origami Whale

Whales are the largest animals that live in the ocean. There are many different **species**, or types, of whales.

The largest species of whale is the blue whale. A blue whale can grow to be about 100 feet (30 m) long. That's longer than a basketball court. An adult blue whale can weigh as much as 30 elephants. These giant animals live in oceans all over the world.

Whales are mammals, which means they are warm-blooded, give birth to live babies, and must breathe air. A whale breathes by coming to the surface of the water and opening and closing a type of nostril called a **blowhole** on top of its head.

YOU WILL NEED:

- To make a whale, one sheet of blue or gray paper
- A marker

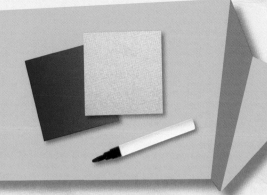

Step 1:

Place the paper colored side down. Fold in half, and crease.

Fold each half into the center crease to create a kite shape, and crease.

Step 2:

Now fold the left-hand point of the kite over, and crease.

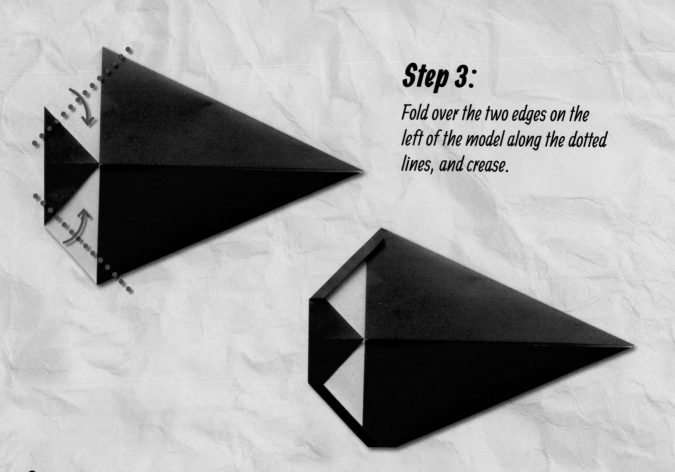

Step 3:

Fold over the two edges on the left of the model along the dotted lines, and crease.

Step 4:

Now fold the model in half along the center crease.

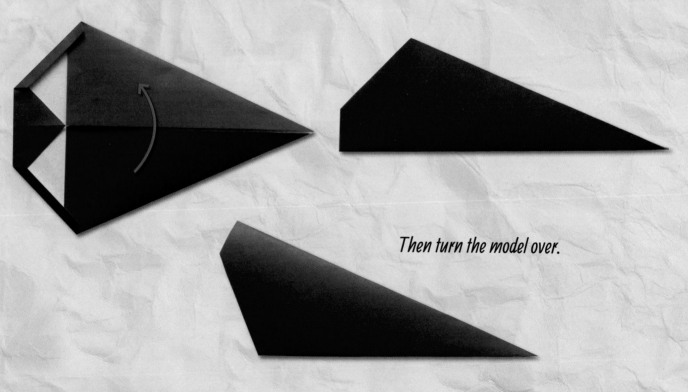

Then turn the model over.

Step 5:

To make the whale's tail, fold in the right-hand point of the model, crease well, and then unfold.

right-hand point

Step 6:

Open out the model. Take hold of the point of the tail and fold it toward the whale's head using the crease you've just made.

Step 7:

Close up the model again, and your whale is complete.

If you wish, you can draw on eyes using a marker. You can also add stick-on, googly eyes.

Open up the whale model slightly so it stands upright.

Origami Dolphin

There are many different species of dolphins.
The best known is the smiley-faced bottlenose dolphin.

These large ocean mammals can grow to be 12.5 feet
(3.8 m) long. Like all mammals, dolphins must breathe air.
A dolphin breathes by swimming to the water's surface
and opening and closing the blowhole on top of its head.

Bottlenose dolphins live in warm oceans around the world in
groups called schools. A school may have just two members,
or as many as a thousand members.

Dolphins are often seen leaping from the water. Scientists
think dolphins do this to send each other messages, such as,
"Let's go!"

Step 1:

Place the paper colored side
down, then fold in half
and crease.

Step 2:

Fold the right-hand
point of the model into
the center, and crease.

Turn the model over, and
fold the new right-hand
point of the model into
the center, and crease.

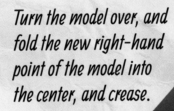

Step 3:

Now slide your fingers into the center "pocket" of the model.
Gently open out the pocket to form a beak-like shape, then
squash the model flat to create a triangle.

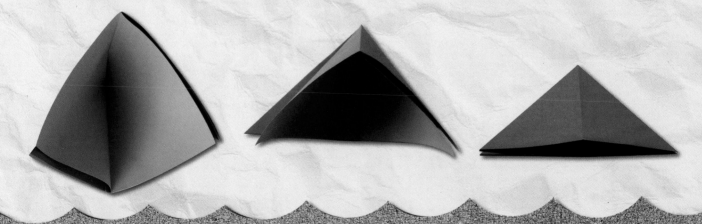

Step 4:

Now take hold of the top layer of paper on the right-hand side of the triangle and fold the point into the center. Crease well, and then unfold.

Step 5:

Take hold of the top layer of paper on the left-hand side and make a fold that follows the line of the crease you made in step 4. Crease well, and then unfold.

Crease made in step 4

Step 6:

Take hold of the top layer of paper on the left-hand side and make a new fold, this time following the line of the crease you made in step 5.

Crease made in step 5

Step 7:

Now make a small fold along the dotted line, and crease well.

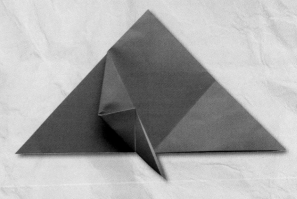

Step 8:

Now fold over the top half of the model along the dotted line.

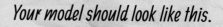

Your model should look like this.

Step 9:

Now fold the center point of the model upward along the dotted line.

Step 10:

Next, fold the left-hand top edge of the model down along the dotted line, and crease well.

Step 11:

Turn the model over. To make the dolphin's tail, take hold of the left-hand point of the model and fold it down and inward as shown.

Next, fold the tip of the tail upward again. The tip will be made of two separate points of paper. Open out the two points to create the dolphin's tail flukes.

The tail should look like this.

Step 12:

To make the dolphin's snout, fold the right-hand point back behind the model, and crease. Then fold the point back toward the right again, creating a small pleat.

Fold the point of the snout behind the model to give the snout a flat end.

Using a marker, draw on an eye.

Dorsal fin

Pleat

Tail flukes

Flipper

snout

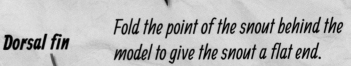

Origami Tropical Fish

The world's oceans are home to thousands of different species of fish. Some of the most colorful fish live on **coral reefs** in **tropical** ocean waters.

Coral reefs are large, underwater, rock-like structures. They are formed from the skeletons of tiny ocean animals called coral polyps. These animals live in **colonies**, joined together by their skeletons. When a polyp dies, its skeleton remains as part of the colony, and over hundreds or thousands of years, a rocky reef forms.

A coral reef habitat is home to thousands of different types of animals, including fish, turtles, crabs, shrimp, sea urchins, and sea sponges. The holes and cracks in a reef are good places to hunt for **prey** or to hide from **predators**.

Step 1:

Place the paper patterned side down. Fold the paper in half, and crease.

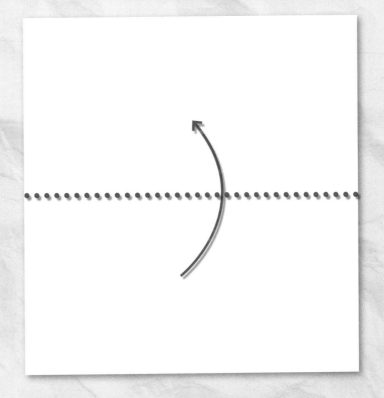

Step 2:

Fold the paper in half again to create a square.

Step 3:

Now open out the square's top layer of paper to create a pocket. Gently squash and flatten the pocket to make a triangle.

Pocket

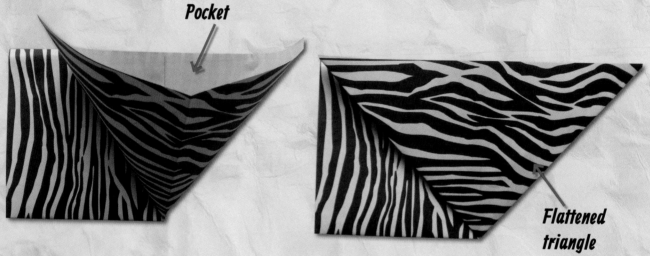

Flattened triangle

Step 4:

Turn the model over. Open out the right-hand side of the model to create a pocket.

Open out here

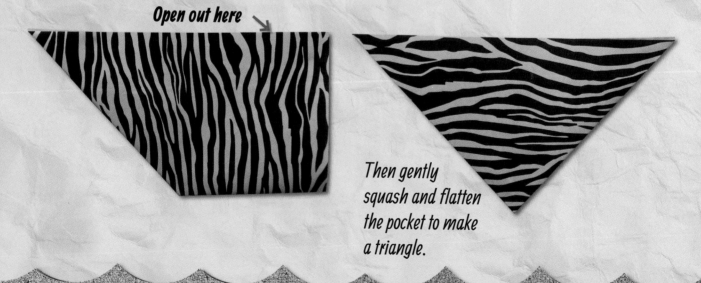

Then gently squash and flatten the pocket to make a triangle.

Step 5:

Turn the triangle on its side. Fold down the top point of the triangle along the dotted line and crease. You should only fold the top layer of paper.

Step 6:

Fold up the bottom point of the model along the dotted line, and crease.

Step 7:

Flip your model over and your tropical fish is complete.

Origami Sea Turtle

Sea turtles are large reptiles that live in oceans around the world. They have four leg-like flippers and a shell. Unlike land turtles, or tortoises, sea turtles cannot pull their heads and flippers into their shells.

There are several different species of sea turtles. Green sea turtles are **herbivores** feeding on seaweed and ocean plants. They get their name from their body fat, which is a greenish color because of the food they eat.

Other species of sea turtles, such as loggerhead and leatherback turtles, are **carnivores** that hunt and eat prey such as jellyfish, crabs, and lobsters.

Step 1:

Place the paper colored side down. Fold in half, and crease.

Fold in half again, and crease.

Step 2:

Now open up the top layer of paper to create a pocket.

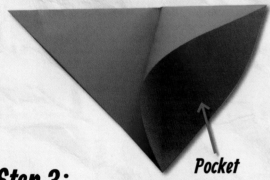

Pocket

Gently squash down the pocket to form a square.

Step 3:

Turn the model over. Open out the triangle-shaped section of the model to create a pocket.

Gently squash down the pocket to form a square.

Open out here

Pocket

Step 4:

Fold in the left- and right-hand sides of the model along the dotted lines, and crease. You should only be folding the top layer of paper.

Step 5:

Fold down the top point of the model, and crease.

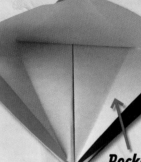

Step 6:

Now open out the folds you made in steps 4 and 5 to create a pocket.

Top point

Pocket

Top point

Take hold of the top point of the pocket and pull it backward while gently squashing and flattening the sides of the pocket to create a diamond shape.

Cut here

Step 7:

Now cut the top half of the diamond through its center along the dotted line.

Step 8:

Fold down the two points of the diamond to create the turtle's front flippers.

Fold and tuck each of the points inside the flippers.

Step 9:

To make the turtle's head, fold the top point of the model backward, and crease hard. Then fold the point forward again, making a small pleat.

Step 10:

Fold out the two bottom points of the model to make the turtle's back flippers.

Head

Pleat

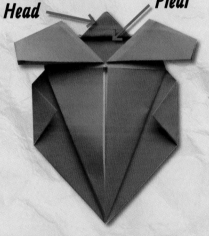

Fold in the two sides of the model to create the turtle's shell.

Step 11:

To make the turtle's tail, fold in the bottom point of the model, and crease. Then fold the point back out again, making a small pleat.

Flip the model over, and it's ready to go!

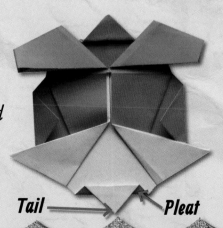

Tail

Pleat

Origami Lobster

The world's oceans are home to many different species of lobsters. These ten-legged creatures belong to a group called **crustaceans** that includes animals such as crabs, crayfish, and shrimp.

Lobsters are **invertebrates**, which means they do not have a skeleton inside their bodies. Instead, they have a hard, outer **exoskeleton**. As a lobster's body grows, its exoskeleton becomes too small and tight. So from time to time, the lobster molts, or sheds, its old, small shell to reveal a new larger shell underneath.

Lobsters hunt for food on the seabed using their long **antennae** to smell for fish, crabs, mussels, and clams.

Step 1:

Place the paper colored side down. Fold in half, crease well, and then unfold.

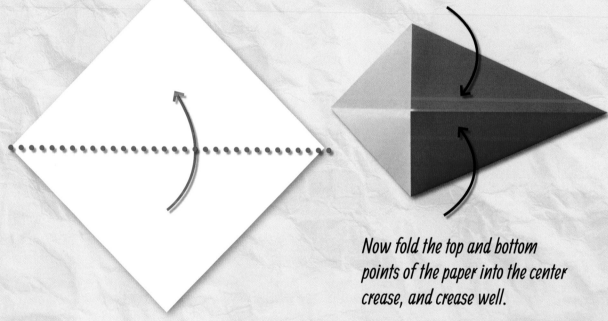

Now fold the top and bottom points of the paper into the center crease, and crease well.

Step 2:

Fold each side of the model into the center crease along the dotted lines, and crease well.

23

Step 3:

Now unfold the creases you made in step 2. Fold the model in half along the center crease, bringing the two outside edges of the model together.

To make the lobster's antennae, cut along the dotted line on the outside edge of the model. Cut through both layers of paper. Do not cut right to the top edge of the model.

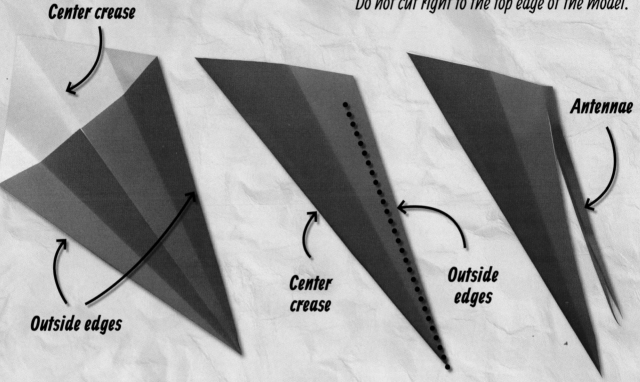

Center crease

Outside edges

Center crease

Outside edges

Antennae

Step 4:

Open out the model again, and fold the two outside edges into the center crease, repeating what you did in step 2. The antennae will now be in the center of the model.

Next, fold the two top points of the model into the center crease, and crease well.

To make the lobster's head, fold the top point of the model down toward the body. Then fold the point back in the opposite direction, making a small pleat.

Fold the two antennae up toward the lobster's head.

Step 6:

To make the lobster's body, fold the bottom half of the model toward the head, and crease. Then fold the bottom half of the model back in the opposite direction, making a small pleat.

Step 7:

Now continue to repeat this step, making pleats all the way down the lobster's body.

Pleats

When the pleats are all made, flip the model over, and the lobster is complete.

Origami Crab

There are thousands of different species of crabs living in oceans worldwide. These ocean creatures come in many sizes, from tiny, dime-sized pea crabs, to giant Japanese spider crabs that can have a legspan of 12 feet (3.7 m).

Like lobsters, crabs are crustaceans. They have an exoskeleton, ten legs, and a pair of large claws, called pincers. Many types of crabs walk sideways.

Crabs feed on lots of different foods, including seaweed, other crustaceans, mussels, sea snails, and worms. Some types of crabs feed on the dead bodies of other ocean animals.

YOU WILL NEED:

• To make a crab, one sheet of colored or patterned paper
• Stick-on googly eyes

Step 1:

Place the paper colored side down. Fold in half, and crease.

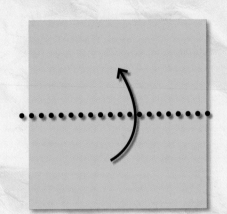

Step 2:

Fold the paper in half again, to make a square.

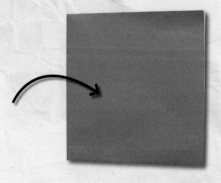

Step 3:

Now open out the square's top layer of paper to create a pocket. Gently squash and flatten the pocket to make a triangle.

Pocket

Flattened triangle

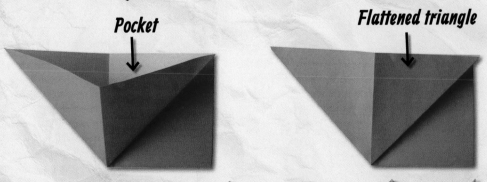

Step 4:

Turn the model over and repeat step 3 by opening out the square end of the model to create a pocket. Then gently squash and flatten the pocket to make a triangle.

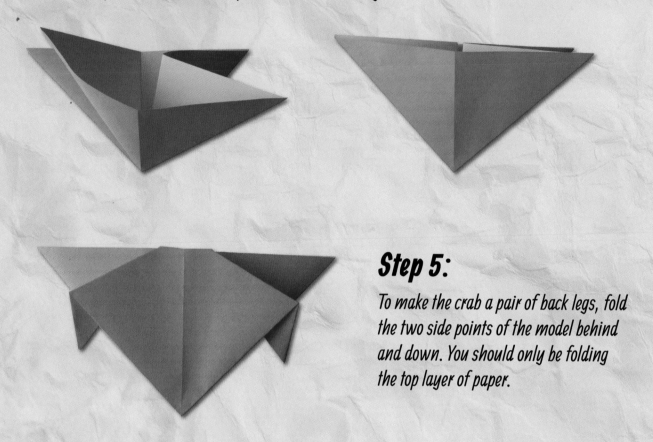

Step 5:

To make the crab a pair of back legs, fold the two side points of the model behind and down. You should only be folding the top layer of paper.

Step 6:

Now fold over the top edge of the model along the dotted line.

Step 7:

To make the crab's front legs and claws, fold each side of the top layer of paper along the dotted lines, and crease well.

Claws

Front leg

Step 8:

Turn the crab over, stick on some googly eyes, and the crab model is finished.

Glossary

antennae (an-TEH-nee)
Long, thin body parts on the heads of some animals including crustaceans and insects.

blowhole (BLOH-hohl)
A nostril-like hole on the head of a whale or dolphin through which the animal breathes.

carnivores (KAHR-neh-vorz)
Animals that eat only meat.

colonies (KAH-luh-neez)
Large groups of living things.

coral reefs (KOR-ul REEFS)
Underwater masses of hard, rocklike matter made from the skeletons of tiny sea animals, called corals, that are joined together. When a coral dies, its skeleton remains, so the mass of coral grows larger and larger.

crustaceans (krus-TAY-shunz)
Invertebrate animals such as lobsters, crabs, and shrimp that have an exoskeleton and jointed legs. Most types of crustacean live in water.

exoskeleton
(ek-soh-SKEH-leh-tun)
The hard outer skeleton of animals such as crustaceans and insects.

habitat (HA-buh-tat)
The place where an animal or plant normally lives. A habitat may be a grassland, the ocean, or a backyard.

herbivores (ER-buh-vorz)
Animals that eat only plants.

invertebrates (in-VER-teh-brets)
Animals that do not have a backbone. Some invertebrates, such as insects and crustaceans, have an exoskeleton. Others, such as worms, slugs, and octopuses have neither an inner skeleton nor an exoskeleton.

mammals (MA-mulz)
Warm-blooded animals that have backbones and usually have hair, breathe air, and feed milk to their young.

origami (or-uh-GAH-mee)
The art of folding paper to make small models. Origami has been popular in Japan for hundreds of years. It gets its name from the Japanese words *ori*, which means "folding," and *kami*, which means "paper."

predators (PREH-duh-turz)
Animals that hunt and kill other animals for food.

prey (PRAY)
An animal that is hunted by another animal as food.

reptiles (REP-tylz)
Animals such as snakes, lizards, turtles, crocodiles, and alligators that are cold-blooded and have scaly skin.

species (SPEE-sheez)
One type of living thing. The members of a species look alike and can produce young together.

tropical (TRAH-puh-kul)
Having to do with the warm areas of Earth near the equator.

For web resources related to the subject of this book, go to:
www.windmillbooks.com/weblinks
and select this book's title.

Read More

McFadzean, Lesley. *Ocean Habitats*. New York: PowerKids Press, 2014.

Schomp, Virginia. *24 Hours on a Coral Reef*. New York: Cavendish Square, 2014.

Shea, Nicole. *Creepy Sea Creatures*. New York: Gareth Stevens, 2012.

Index